R

Worth

Jaye Little

Cover Design by Demetrius Clarke |
Clarke Creative Agency
Front Cover Photo by
Ashley VictoriaLens Photography
Editor:
Sonya Taylor

DEDICATION

I am honored to dedicate this book to all of my mothers, sisters, aunts, nieces, cousins, "babygirls," mentees, and friends, who simply just need a push to become ALL of who God has called them to be.

Remember: YOU ARE WORTHY! <3

I especially dedicate this book to my scholars at Jefferson Davis High School in Montgomery, Alabama.
I love y'all SO MUCH.

#AHopeToHelp
#FYP
"For The Young People"

I want you to know how IMPORTANT your story is. Many of you do not speak up enough, but you literally hold keys to the next level for somebody else. <u>Many times we experience things, handle them privately, and then do not help the next person going through a similar situation. NEWSFLASH: Everything that you go through is to help somebody else. That is why I am writing this to you, now, as we speak.</u>

Your story– every single detail– is needed for where God is taking you. Don't back down. Don't let the enemy intimidate you. Don't allow fear to hold you back. We don't know what anyone else is going through out here, so it's important that we focus on our own personal growth and be authentic. No one can beat you at being you. Therefore, GO FOR IT ALL!

-   Miss Jaye from A Hope To Help

CONTENTS

ACKNOWLEDGMENTS

I must acknowledge all speakers and panelists who participated in the #RestoreHerWorth Conference of 2021. I believe that it changed our lives for the better.

Monique Waugh
LaTrice Zimmerman
Danielle Sykes
Brianca Hardy
Tammie Brooks
Jessica Smith
Brooklyn Jenkins
Trinity Chukwuma
Keiondra Moon
Olivia Raife
Alani White
Thailyn Rogers
Brittany Miles
Taylor White
Z'Karia Marshall
Alexandra Lopez
A'leya Smith

To the sponsors and volunteers, THANK YOU.

"The more that she poured.
The more that she gave.
The more that she tried.
The more that she allowed.
The more that she tolerated.
The more that she was disrespected,
rejected, and abandoned.
The more that she lost herself in others
by living for them and not herself.

**AT LAST, the cycle stops here.
IT STOPS NOW.
THIS WILL NOT BE HER
STORY, ANYMORE."**

- Jayelisa M. Little

Let's Face It

Do YOU even like YOU?

If you looked at yourself in the mirror right now undressed with no hair extensions, makeup, or jewelry, **would you be satisfied with what YOU SEE?**

If you couldn't even answer that question with a sure "YES!," then you need to be here. Loving you all starts with you and **you can't expect anybody to love you if you don't love yourself, first.** How horrible is that? To expect someone to do what you don't have the capacity to do is NOT FAIR.

Before we even get into friendships, relationships, and situationships, let's start with you. This book title doesn't say, "Restore Their

Worth." We're focusing on the "HER," and the "HER" is "YOU." Well…it's "US" but you get what I'm saying. Lol

ANYWAY!

Please note that this book is going to be written how I talk and everything will not be perfectly grammatical. It's going to be as if we are sitting on the porch having a "Come To Jesus" Meeting concerning how we treated ourselves and how we allowed others to treat us.

IT'S TIME OUT FOR THE BULLCRAP that we have settled for. I'm not here to waste time with you, friend. I'm here to push you to WIN. The way that we have looked at ourselves without knowing our identity in Christ is absolutely disgusting. The way that we have treated others, especially women, due to our own insecurities is heartbreaking, as well. The way that we have allowed people to mishandle us all for the sake of acceptance, validation, approval, comfort, or whatever false reality we tried to create and hold onto **IS NO LONGER ACCEPTABLE.**

People treat you how you let them treat you, and your life will always reflect how you view yourself. The question is:

WHAT DO YOU SEE WHEN YOU LOOK AT YOURSELF IN THE MIRROR?
We must answer this question first!

We must also answer these, too:

Does how you see yourself come from something that has happened to you?
Or from what someone else has called you?
Is there a word that shouts out from what someone said to you a long time ago, or even recently?
How do you label yourself?
Ugly?
Fat?
Ho?
B*tch?
Slut?
Dumb?
T.H.O.T.?
Insecure?
Bimbo?
Disappointment?

Mistake?
Easy?
Skinny?
Messy?
Trash?
Skank?
Whore?
Worthless?
Useless?
Disgusting?
Never Be Anything?
Only Good Enough To Lay On Your Back?
[Did I hit home, yet?]

Are these words that you attached to yourself along the years of growing up and you just started to wear and own them for yourself?

Well....let's unpack it all.
That's why you are here, right?

Get you a journal, girl. It is so necessary to **document your progress.** Write down your thoughts, and most importantly, be true to yourself. Be honest and transparent; it's the only way that we can get healed.

You have this book because you feel that there is a missing piece that must be identified, faced, and conquered. My prayer is that we grow together as sisters on this journey of getting back to knowing our worth, standing firm on our morals and standards, and never settling for less, EVER AGAIN.

Let's go.

Comparison Kills

Worth will never be found in what you do, who you're with, where you go, or how you look. It is not measured by how well you can handle life's trials or how good of a mother you may be.

Your worth was already determined and ordained by God and if we really take a glimpse of how He sees us, then we will gain a bigger insight on how we see ourselves.

Some of the main things that eat at our worth are:
- comparison
- **self-doubt**
- comparison

- **self-harm**
- comparison
- **allowing others to mistreat you, continuously**
- comparison
- **not speaking up**
- comparison
- **fear**
- comparison
- **no standards/boundaries/morals**

and most importantly, **<u>COMPARISON!</u>**

Now class, what is one thing that eats at our worth? *waits for an answer*

Did you say, "comparison"?

Okay! Very good!

Chile!

How many times did we feel that we were not enough simply by looking at what someone else had going on in their life and trying to keep up with them?

I never liked competitions because they are

only based on the opinions and approval of other people– and that's the last thing that we should be worried about– another person's opinion. Now, I'm not talking about sporting events and time record gatherings. I'm referring to image-based competitions.

Society spends a lot of time trying to tell us how we should look, what we should wear, how we should speak, where we should go, and what size we should be. Meanwhile, society has never provided us with anything such as money, transportation, or utilities to get to any level that it tells us about. **SOCIETY DID NOT CREATE US.** Therefore, there is no need to spend time scrolling, searching, sulking, and complaining about things that we may or may not have. Society doesn't give us life, and it definitely can't take it away, unless it is allowed. Society only opens doors for us to compare our lives to what it displays.

Comparing ourselves to other people, in my opinion, is such an insult to God. If He wanted us to be them, wouldn't He have created us that way? Please understand everything about us: the way that we were made, our hair, our eyes, our shape, our size, our gifts, our talents, our characteristics, our sound, our visions, our dreams, etc. God intentionally made us this way ON PURPOSE. I can't sit here and act like I've never been displeased with myself about things that I can't change. However, I had to humble myself and thank God for it all. There are people out here who may not have the very thing that we complain about having, and it shows how ungrateful we are, sometimes. We all have a reason to be grateful. At this point, just being able to see another day is a blessing for me.

After humbling myself, I had to ask God to help me accept how He made me. There are things about us that we will never be able to change. Acceptance comes from within, but it's birthed from knowing that God made us all fearfully and wonderfully.

Everything about you is on purpose. You may think that you're "too this," or "too that." However, God says, " No, you're just right. I knew exactly what I was doing when I made you that way. Don't sleep on yourself. That exact thing that you're displeased about, I'm still pleased about it and I'm going to use it for My glory. It's all a part of My plan for you."

<u>Moral: You can't be compared to anyone because **YOU ARE INCOMPARABLE.**</u>

BREAK IT DOWN

I know that I mentioned a few things that could eat at your worth in the last section. However, we eat on our own worth more than we think. While the enemy does all that it can to make sure that we think that our lives don't matter, we too can also play a big part in not maintaining the worth that God gave us when He created us.

Self - Sabotage

These are thoughts and behaviors that hinder and prevent us from doing what we want to do. It's saying, thinking, and believing "I can't do this," and "I'm not good enough." If we don't think well of ourselves or are constantly displeased with our actions, this can lead us to self-sabotaging ourselves. If we have people around us who usually question and criticize our actions or sayings as if it is an issue, we may develop a tendency to just stop moving or talking all at once, in order to not "be a burden to others." This could develop habits of self-sabotage, as well. Self-sabotage is literally putting a stop sign right in front of ourselves, and it robs us of new and great opportunities, connections, and experiences in life.

Doubting God

Doubting God can be from a root of many things. We may have developed trust issues from our friend and/or family relationship experiences, and that'll create a tough space to even trust God. It's hard to trust someone you can't see when you constantly have issues with the ones that you can see.

When we generally do not believe or have a sense of hope, that blocks high self-esteem for ourselves, **automatically.** Also, when we don't trust God and God's plan for our life, when He is the one that created us, we will set ourselves up for failure, **everytime.**

Knowing who God is, by reading His Word, and believing in who God is concerning our life will always keep us in the vein of worth because we have a true understanding of who we are.

Doing It Yourself (An "I Got This" Attitude)

This refers to a level of pride, thinking that we only know what's best for us. To think that we don't need help or guidance in this life will always humble us in a way that we will never forget. We must crawl before we walk. Remember that our worth is never defined by what we do, but by Who created us. Our life is a gift from God.

Tolerating Disrespect/Abuse

Now, this is one of the ultimate things that just destroys and kills our worth. When we know that the words or actions of someone toward us are out of line, and we continue to allow it to happen, not only do we not know our worth, but we are teaching others the cost of our worth. We must speak up, be honest about times when we are being mistreated, and do whatever is necessary to exit stage left. We don't deserve such treatment– especially when we have God who loves and protects us. We should expect nothing less from human interaction.

Negative Language

Now…we all are guilty of this. Carrying low self-esteem will cause us to "down talk" ourselves in the worst form. Sometimes we'll even downplay ourselves before someone else ever has the chance to. Not only do we slander ourselves, but we have the nerve to talk about others, too! **Anyone who fixes their mouth to talk about anybody else is insecure, and needs to shut their mouth–all the way.** No one has room to downgrade a soul because no one is perfect and we all have made mistakes that we don't want mentioned. It is time to change our language and speak life.

Not Praying

Talking to God is important. When we are not honest, open, transparent, and vulnerable to God, it can be difficult to see ourselves the way that He sees us. Prayer is a conversation with God that says, " I trust you with the innermost parts of me." When we do not communicate with our Creator as the creation, we hinder our growth and knowledge of who He really is in our lives.

Being Wishy-Washy/Fickle

The best thing that we could ever have is a made up mind. When we don't know what we want, or when we go back and forth from one decision to another– that's a playing ground for the enemy to confuse us. When we don't know who we are, it's hard to have any idea of what kind of decision to make, including knowing what our worth is. We must take the time out to be still and prioritize our thoughts and moves.

Allowing Emotions To Control You

We let our feelings get the best of us, sometimes, and it's really sad. By allowing our emotions to control us, we can block blessings and promotions, forfeit a learning moment, and miss an opportunity to reconcile with friends. When we let anger, rage, bitterness, jealousy, and envy takeover, it's not going to look good when interacting with anyone. Emotions can usually cloud us from facing the truth and hinder us from being productive. Trust me, I know. However, let's pay attention to how many times our emotions have stopped us from moving forward, accomplishing goals, and working to the best of our ability. It's okay to acknowledge your feelings and take a moment, but don't let them paralyze you from living life. **Take control.**

Trying To Please Everyone Else

Oh, boy! This was a tough one for me. Making yourself available for so many people and never taking time out for yourself is one of the biggest ways to lose you. When you're focusing on pleasing everyone else, your morals are low and you haven't figured out what you need to be doing with your life yet. Spend some time away and get to know you, even if you don't like you, yet. It's not safe to show up for everyone except for yourself. And let me say this, now: **Never wait on somebody else to validate you. If you are alive, then you're already validated.**

Lying To Yourself & Believing The Lies

This could be as simple as saying, "I'm okay," when YOU KNOW THAT YOU ARE NOT OKAY. This is when we wear a poker face (always smiling) but in reality, we're really hurting inside because we haven't told ourselves THE TRUTH. Sometimes we can know the truth, but we don't face the truth. Anytime that we don't face our truth, we're choosing to lie to ourselves and remain in bondage. There are people out here who can help us sort out our thinking to acknowledge the difference between the truth and a lie within our lives. Being in denial about ourselves is unacceptable. We should tell ourselves the truth.

Do you see yourself in some of the above descriptions? I understand; we have all been there. However, now that you know, I'm holding you responsible. In all, be accountable for your actions, take care of yourself, and do not be deceived by your own feelings.

Ready for more?

Build It Up (W.O.W.)

This book won't be too long because the work for our worth is up to us. Our journey is always determined by what we will allow and what we won't allow. Since we're here, we may as well let God do His good work in us, for us, and through us.

While it took me a minute to be bold enough to even write this book to you(us), I'm so glad that we are finally here. Along with opening up to God and allowing Him to clean and restore us, it's important that we are careful with how we carry ourselves throughout life. In this section, I will refer to us as "Women of Worth" or let's just say this: W.O.W. = Woman of Worth

Keep Your Name Clean

I'm not sure if you've heard of the saying, "Don't let your good be evil spoken of." However, keeping your name clean is a very important deal as a woman. In this book, keeping your name clean means that you are kind to all people, not spending time entertaining drama and gossiping about people, and not having sex with a number of people at the same time. Keeping our name clean keeps doors and opportunities open for us. **What is your reputation like?** A W.O.W. is not going to allow herself to be in the company of so many boys or men that it'll appear to be that she is an "around the way" girl or " for the streets." While the statement may not be true about you, it's just a thought that I want you to keep in mind. While the world is definitely foul, mean, cruel, and nowadays, opportunities can come just by knowing someone, a W.O.W. standard should never be compromised for any promotion. **If you give your body in order to receive acceptance, then it's not worth having.**

Are you always around people who are fighting or involved in a lot of gossip groups and group chats? I will just say be careful about what you say. Anyone that can bring you a bone(someone else's tea) can also take a bone(your tea), too. I've seen a few situations where running your mouth about someone else's business doesn't put you in a good place with friends. I've been involved in a few gossip groups and have been guilty by association, even if I didn't say anything about the person. However, because I listened and allowed it to happen, I was just as bad as the people talking.

I have also trusted the wrong people with sensitive information about me and what I said came back to me through someone else. It's just not a good vibe to always have someone else's name in your mouth, especially when the news is about something that doesn't concern you. **If you're not going to help them, then don't talk about them. Everybody has dirt.**

Most importantly, when you choose not to gossip or shut it down as soon as you hear it, unless it's a lie, then your name will not be mentioned when the mess starts to grow. It's just best to keep your mouth off of other people. Be kind to people. It'll go a long way. "Treat people how you want to be treated." This is a good way to keep your name clean.

Cut The Soul Ties

Now most of us, if not all, have experienced being connected to someone that WE KNOW we shouldn't be connected to, right? Some of us may have even had sex with someone that's not our husband, but we still can't get the man out of our heads. We've spent time trying to get them out of our minds, but something, even them, just keeps pulling us back to them. I will tell you this: **IT WILL HURT WORSE IF YOU DON'T LET GO, NOW.**

By now, you probably already know that he isn't the one. He doesn't even treat you well. You may only still be there because you know that you love him. If you're honest with yourself, you know that it's time to say goodbye. This is one of the hardest things that I've had to do, over and over again, with multiple young men because they had an emotional and mental tie with me, and I never had sex with the young men– they just got into my head enough. I allowed it because I didn't know my worth, girl. However, when you want better and you're tired of the same cycles, something has to break. I had to ask God to help me break free, and by reading His Word, learning how to make up my mind and say, "No," I was eventually able to get out of there. Now, your story may be different– I'm sure that it is. However, if you know that it's time to go, let's make it happen. **You deserve better.**

Make Sound Decisions

Y'all, when I decided to "mean what I say and say what I mean," life became so much simpler for me. Usually, we all know when we are making the right decisions, and we also know when we aren't. As a W.O.W., we don't have the time to make decisions that will hinder us from being great in our future. It's simple: "Do right and right will follow you." Make up your mind on what kind of person you want to be in character, and then dominate. **Will we make mistakes? YES. However, just don't make the same mistakes again and again.**

Accept Your Mistakes and Forgive You

Sometimes, we are really hard on ourselves and sometimes we are just too comfortable. At times we may fall really short and have no knowledge of how to get back up. When we don't try to do better from the mistakes that we made, this is when we sell ourselves short. I've experienced thinking about a mistake that I made a long time ago, and just getting mad all over again, at myself. The situation was over, I forgave the other person, but I didn't forgive myself and it stopped me from moving forward in freedom. Most of the time, we hold our own selves back due to fear and not wanting to make a mistake, again. However, when you trust God and His plan for you, realize that **you are forgiven** and every new day that you're given is another opportunity to get it right, then you will succeed. It's all about changing your mindset. You have to believe in God and then believe what He says about you.

Breathe After The Break Up

Too many times, we tend to rebound men right after another. When one leaves us, or when we leave one, we feel that we must fill in that space to occupy the time that was once for someone else. Do you know how damaging it can be to not heal from one relationship and drag the damage into another one? It's not fair to the other person to have to deal with something that you should've handled before getting into a new relationship. When you breathe after the break up, it simply gives you space to heal, regroup, cry, pray, focus, and just be free. Once all of that has taken place, then you will be ready to receive anyone that comes your way without being bitter, hurt, and broken.

Rest In The Arms Of God More Than The Arms Of Man

I'm not sure if you know this or not, but man will always fail you whether it's intentionally, or unintentionally. By **man(biblically; not gender specific)**, I mean your friends, your family, and your relationships. Whenever we want someone to be there for us when we need them, sometimes, it doesn't seem like they are available all of the time. **God is the only one who knows exactly what we feel, what we are thinking, and how to heal us.** However, we have to develop our perspective of God as a friend and a comforter. While it's good to have a physical person there with us to hold us and hug us, we need to be realistic and know that that's a vulnerable space and we are susceptible to being taken advantage of in moments like that. **Trust God with your emotions, first, and then He will lead you to who you can be vulnerable with in due time.**

I THOUGHT THAT I LOST

My life has gone through a lot of ups and downs in friendships, relationships, and situationships. Not only has my life gone through many things, but I've taken myself through many of those downs all because I did not embrace my worth in God. I have a beautiful family who tells me about my worth and says how beautiful I am, but if I never believe it for myself, then everything that they say will always be null and void. I have blamed everything and everyone around me for what has happened in my life, but do you know what I didn't do? **I did not take responsibility for my own actions.**

For years, I literally used to blame not having my biological father around for the guys that I attracted and were attracted to, but I failed to understand that after a couple of mess ups and falls, that it was no longer my Daddy's fault– IT WAS ME. I had a problem and I needed to face my truth.

Y'all, I spent years settling for guys who didn't want me, but I still wanted to prove my love to them in hopes that they would accept me. I missed great opportunities with great men because I still had baggage from soul ties. I have spent years tolerating, attracting, and healing broken men, all to still be single, today. Side note: There is still purpose in my singleness, right now. That is why I am able to write this book to you.

The truth is: HURT PEOPLE HURT PEOPLE. While I know this to be true, it was evident in my pattern of situationships. I have been rejected and mishandled a number of times…so much that I grew the characteristics of the guys who hurt my feelings. I ended up mishandling guys, ghosting them, using them, and rejecting them, too. It is all a cycle. The enemy wants you to be hurt, so that you will not grow a true relationship with God, get to know yourself, and be a vessel of love how you were created to be.

While I tell a little bit of my story as if it is a sad story…**there is always a big miracle that comes out of a big mess.** This is Jaye. I am currently a 26-year old virgin who is speaking with you, right now. You can't ask me how I made it here, because I have NO IDEA. You are talking to someone who has been with, hung around, dated, partied with, and loved a NUMBER of guys and men, BUT for some reason, the Lord did not allow me to have sexual intercourse with NAN ONE OF THEM. After having experienced sooooo many guys who either enjoyed my company, wanted to be with me because of what I had, or because of my connections, none of them stayed around because they wanted to have sex with me and I vowed not to before getting married. Now, have I almost crossed that line? Yes, but now that I know God and I love Him, I only want to do what pleases Him. Sex before marriage, along with other sins, will not get us to where we need to be in the Kingdom of God, let alone know the full value of our worth. **It is not easy, but I know that it will be worth it.** I tried drinking, smoking, and a list of other things "of" this world. **The miracle is that God kept me.**

Some of you may not be virgins, but you can submit your body back to Christ until your husband comes. That is one of our issues, now: we submit so much to guys too early and to those that have nothing to give us in return. Women give soooo much to people. We give our time, money, bodies, and so many other things to people who are only there to just take, take, and take. **That's not fair to us.** I am not saying that having sex with people means that you do not know your worth, but why not be with someone who knows that you are worth the wait, rather than using you for sex and then move on to the next person? You deserve more, and so do they, but none of us really know it, yet. Let's get back to the saying: **People treat you how you allow them to treat you.**

What I learned throughout all of those men that I encountered is that they were never ready for me, as a woman of worth. I was not ready for them, either. I didn't even know what my worth was; I only had one rule: **I am not having sex before marriage**.

I literally did everything else. From kissing to fondling(touching), but they did not like the fact that I had a "lock down" on sexual intercourse. For the ones who tried me, they thought that I was "easy," and they thought that if they told me, "I love you," then I would eventually give in…To be honest….I am so glad that I didn't because I wouldn't be writing this book to you now… Imagine how crazy I would've been if I did have sex with them…LORD HAVE MERCY.

The miracle is that God protected me from what could have taken me all the way OUT. He has a bigger plan for me. This whole time throughout my situationships, I thought that God did not want me to have a significant other, or be happy with someone as my boyfriend or husband.

Meanwhile, during those times, I was not aware of my worth and I settled for anybody that came my way. God does not operate in confusion, and He will not allow anything to come into your life that will take you away from Him. God is a jealous God and there shall be no other Gods before Him.

NO FRIENDSHIP/RELATIONSHIP WILL WORK OUT IF GOD IS NOT THE CENTER OF IT.

Now that I have a greater understanding of

who God is in my life, where I am supposed to be, and who I am assigned to, I'm grateful to be here on this journey with you. **When God keeps you, He keeps you for a reason. So, just be grateful for the things that did not work out, because God has something BETTER AHEAD.**

Before we go, I have to give you **The Four S's.**

The 4 S's are things that a W.O.W. SHOULD NOT SETTLE FOR IN CONNECTIONS AND SITUATIONSHIPS. Notice how I didn't say friendships and relationships. If there is any time that you feel that you are one of these, GET OUT OF THAT ENTANGLEMENT, NOW. Whether you know it or not, you are worth more than that.

[THE Four S's]
Woman of Worth, you should not allow a boy/guy/man to have you as a:

- **Side Piece**
- **Second Option**
- **Sneaky-Link**
- **Secret**

THE FOUR S'S

These four sayings are words that I have actually participated in, back in my day, and they are the definition of "not knowing your worth." I can't tell you how many times I've settled for being just the girl who was okay with getting a text, and if I'm lucky, a call only on the weekdays and not the weekends or even vice versa. I can't tell you how many times I was okay with flirting with a guy who I knew had a girlfriend, and actually entertained them, thinking that I was the special one. I can't tell you how many times I've been told or it has been assumed that they don't want to be seen with me in public, only in my place and barely their place. I can't tell you how many times I was okay with guys coming to find me to spend time with me and get emotionally healed because they were in their feelings about what they were going through in life, and was never ever asked, "Well Jaye, how are you doing?"

Y'all I have the right to talk about these four sayings. I have this joke when I say, " I used to be the CEO of the Side-Chick Service Systems," and as much as I didn't know my worth looking back at my past, IT HAD TO BE TRUE.

Now, I do not praise any of these sayings. Representing these sayings is what broke me, made me have bitter feelings toward people, lose my worth, and almost lose my life, y'all. When you don't know who you are, you will fall for anything. **When you can't see the beautiful woman when you look in the mirror, it's a scary standpoint because it is an open door for the devil to deceive you of your image. When you can't see what God sees in you, you're clouded from the truth.**

Look at them for a moment, and then conduct a self inventory. If you see something that may mirror your lifestyle, just decide on what you want to do next. Remember that all information that you're exposed to, you're responsible for it.

Side Piece

A side piece is when a woman is dating a man

and she knows that he either has a main girlfriend or a wife. The woman is aware that the man is with someone else, but she is content in being the lady on the side for sexual pleasure, extra company, or other things.

Second Option

A second-option is just that– NOT THE FIRST CHOICE. Usually a woman is the second option when the man turned down the woman the first time to be with someone else, but when it didn't work out with them, he decided to return and work things out with her.

Sneaky-Link

A sneaky-link is when two people may or may not have significant others–that's not always the case– but they decide to meet together for sexual pleasure, without telling anyone anything. They are, or should be, the only two that know about the link up. Sneaky-links can simply be sex-buddies, and that's it. No commitment for later. Just sex.

Secret

This right here is when a guy wants sex, dates,

and time from you, but doesn't want anyone to know that you all are seeing each other. They don't want you to post them on your social media pages; they definitely don't post you. They only suggest meeting out of town, rather than locally. They may say " I don't like people all in my business," or " Don't tell anyone that we are together." Y'all, it's horrible. This isn't for protection for you; it's just for them. You definitely are not the only woman that he's seeing either. **Too much secrecy can lead to deception. There is nothing wrong with the truth.**

As I was defining these titles, so many emotions flared up… because how many of us have had one of these titles, or knows someone who does, right now?

This is unacceptable. As women of worth, we must treat ourselves better than this. We are worth so much more than being any of the names mentioned above. I really pray that we all come to terms with our identity in Christ, our worth in Christ, and do whatever it takes to treat ourselves better as we expect those around us to do the same.

I want to share with you one of my most

recent conversations that I had with a man that I ghosted last year, some time. We had been on and off about four different times for about two years until I decided to finally cut it out. **The truth is, I allowed him to return time and time again, knowing that he wasn't the man that God sent as my husband, all because I enjoyed the attention and I really didn't walk in my worth as a woman.** I knew that I didn't want him for the right reasons; but for some reason, he kept coming back around and I allowed him to. Before this time, during one of our last conversations, I opened up to him about a weakness that I was personally dealing with and he mentioned that he wished that he could've taken advantage of that moment. I told him that I desired sex at a certain time and he said that he should've caught me in that moment so that he could have sex with me. That's all. Nothing too crazy. Lol

Nevertheless, this conversation happened literally between 2021-2022 on Dec. 31 and Jan 1st. The devil tried to distract me already for the new year! He reached out to me before, but I ignored him. However, after having a nice dream about him(the devil's deception tactic), I decided to accept the friend request that he sent me on

Facebook…again. Don't judge me. I had him blocked on my phone and unfriended him on all social media, so to contact me, he had to send another friend request. LOL.

Dec 9, 2021

Him:
Hello ma'am. I hope all is well with you.

I'll be in Montgomery in December. If you want to hang out let me know.

Dec 31, 2021
*accepts friend request."
Him: Hey

Me: Good evening. Are you available to speak on the phone for a moment?
Him: Give me a few minutes. I'm leaving my brother house. Give me your number and I'll call you
Me: I'll call you when you're available.
Him: Ok
Me: I won't be available to talk tonight. I'm preparing to sing for a service. Would you like to catch up tomorrow?
Him: I'm leaving now……Was that you?
Me: Yes.
Him: Ok bet. Because I don't have your number.
Me: I figured that. Hence why I called.

When we talked on the phone, I apologized to him for ghosting him, and told him the reason why I did. He didn't like talking on the phone, but I did. He only likes texting, so one day when I asked him what he was up to, he texted back and said, "on the phone," so I then blocked him, because I was upset and childish. Lol. We didn't stay on the phone too long because he kept putting me on hold and since I had to sing for a service, I went on and hung up. Now, Let's move on to the rest of the text messages.

Him: Will you be available to text
Me: Hey. No Sir. Not tonight.
Him: Ok

January 1, 2022 12:39am (just got out of service)
Me: Happy New Year
Him: Happy New Years ….Wake up
Me: Oh I'm awake
Him: What are you doing? .. I'm shocked you up. Talking about noooo. I'm not be able to text tonight.
Me: Eating taco soup and chips. .. It's morning, now. I said what I said.
Him: Yo ahh about to be gassy af. Good thing I ain't there to smell these bombs your dropping lol
Me: Well thank you! Lol I don't mind.
Him: Lol. I bet. .. So how was your performance tonight?
Me: Service was great, tonight. Thank you for asking.
Him: No problem. So I'm assuming you did your thang on the 1s and 2s.

Me: God was pleased. It was awesome!

Him: That's awesome. Well I'm glad you did a great job and enjoyed yourself.

Me: Thank you so much, Sir.

Him: You're so welcome ma'am. .. Now you finally decided to add me back lol

Me: Eh, not quite. Is there a reason why you still reach out to me? Even after several times of fall backs? Why?

Him: I told you what's up a long time ago. Regardless we always gone be friends no matter what.

You're good people and I f*cks with you heavy because of that. So no matter what I'm gone always be in the picture. Might not be how you pictures it but regardless I'm gone always be here.

Me: I'm still trying to answer why I'm mean to you and no one else... really. Lol .. Even if I push you away, huh? .. Why do you even want to be here?.. Well here only via text lol

Him: You mean to me because you like me.

You push me away in hopes that's gone solve the issue when it's not.

I want to be here because you a kind hearted person. Despite of our past you overall have a very pure heart and you an awesome person. I choose to stick around.

Cut me some slack. I'm a texter because I told you why lol. But I'm working on that. ..

Plus no lie you a whole vibe. So I like your energy. Even when you attempt to be mean I laugh..

Plus because you love my smile lol

Me: "But I'm working on that." 📝
Him: *sends me a picture of him smiling*
Me: You gotta get over yourself, (Name).
Him: Nawl. It's the truth. Where the lies?
Me: Everywhere. I'm just not interested in you like that, anymore.
Him: That's understandable. Well hopefully our friendship can last. If not, I understand.
Me: It does take 2. However, besides flirting and texting, that's all that we had, at first. .. I'll work on my end
Him: I think you be so caught up in the fact we text that you miss the fact we still constantly communicate. Regardless how we communicate I still talked to you all the time.

Yea we flirt and stuff like that. Regardless that's gone always be there.

At this point, I decide to go to bed and then respond in the morning. I could have just ignored him, but I didn't want to ghost him, again, so here's where we get to the root.

Jan 1, 2022 8:06am
Me: Good Morning, (Name).
When texting, one will never be able to fully

understand what a person is truly saying, because EFFECTIVE COMMUNICATION comes when you listen to the tone of the person, when they say it, how they say it, and feel the energy that's transferred to the other person when the statement is made. Digital communication destroys true human interaction and it confuses feelings/emotions. I could think about something that you said through text, get mad about it, but when we finally talk about it, you didn't even mean it that way. That's unnecessary.

Our communication is not effective. It has never been effective. Every time we've talked, its about the same thing. Whether it was God vs. Sex, Text vs. Talk, Freaky Talk vs. Non Freaky Talk.
It's not one sided. I've had my moments, too.
I apologize for anything that I may have done to disrespect you, make you feel less of a man, and to make you feel that you aren't enough. You are enough in God's eyes.

Just texting you, even as a friend, is not enough, when you've chosen not to consider that THIS FRIEND likes to communicate verbally. In friendship there's consideration and simple care. There's accountability and unselfishness. I shouldn't have to just be okay with how YOU like to text, and you haven't once said, " Well let me meet my friend half way, or something since she likes to talk."

Consistency means nothing if there's no growth. Our "friendship"(connection) hasn't grown or evolved since meeting. On both sides.

Like I mentioned, as well as I should, you have to get over yourself. And that's what's I've learned to do this year(2021), for me.

And what's best for me is if we no longer communicate. I THANK YOU for your time, the energy that you take to even reach out to me. It's thoughtful of you.
However, I'd rather move on, completely, without communicating.

I pray that you understand. I pray that you hear my heart. I hope that all is well.

Maybe you will find a friend who's okay with only texting you. I'm just not that friend, and I don't want to be that friend.

Can we agree, or agree to disagree, and separate peacefully, (Name)?

I also sent him a voice message, saying similar things, but I think that you get the gist of it. Long story short, I told him that our friendship was stagnant and we both deserved better, and I asked if we could just move on from one another.

Him: Bet

I shared this with you, because I need you to understand that when you realize that enough is enough, you'll make up your mind and start making some changes about yourself and the people around you will start to see it, too. **BE WHAT YOU WANT TO SEE.** When you treat yourself better, God will send the right people around you that'll treat you well, too. **YOU ARE WORTHY. NEVER SETTLE FOR LESS.**

DO THE WORK!

In this section, I am creating the blueprint of where to start in our worth being restored. I am a person who believes that **when you do the work, results will show up.** For seven to eight years, I've settled for less, mishandled my own self, dishonored God, and today, I have vowed to never do that again. My prayer is that you make that same vow, too. I deserve more. You deserve more. This is just the beginning. <u>**Woman of Worth, carry out your assignment. Someone needs the FULL YOU. You CAN DO THIS!**</u>

1. God needs to be NUMBER ONE in your life.

I apologize that I can't accommodate you with practical steps without the guidance of God, but then again, I can't apologize. This is how I'm making it, and I'm only here to share my journey with you. If you find a different outlet, go for it. However, I believe that all roads lead to God, no matter what.

As you make the decision to have God in your life and put Him back in place as head of your life, you're going to need something to back it up– His Word– The HOLY BIBLE.

Here are some scriptures to be introduced to in your journey:

- **Philippians 3:12-14**
- **Song of Solomon 4:7**
- **Proverbs 31**
- **Psalm 46:5**
- **Jeremiah 29:11**
- **1 Peter 3:3-4**
- **Luke 12:6-7**
- **2 Timothy 1:7**
- **Ephesians 1**
- **Romans 12:2**
- **Jeremiah 1:5**
- **Matthew 6:26**
- **Romans 8: 35, 37**
- **1 Peter 5:7**
- **Proverbs 3:11-12**
- **Romans 8:28**
- **John 3:16**
- **Galatians 6:9**
- **1 Peter 2:9**
- **2 Corinthians 12:9**
- **James 4:8**

2. The Mirror Task

Take a few hours out of your day for this.

Materials: A big mirror, a marker, post-it papers, and a Bible with a dictionary and concordance

- Look at yourself in the mirror for a while.
- Write down everything that you see onto the mirror with your marker. (How you feel when you see yourself, any words that pop up in your head, and labels that you've been given over the years). This is harder than it sounds. However, do your best to write it out.
- After you write those words, you will use post-its to counteract every negative word that you wrote with a positive statement. For example: If you wrote "ugly" on the mirror, your post-it note can say, "I am beautiful and I love the way that I look." To my bible readers, look up a scripture that counteracts the negative terms that you write on the mirror. For example, if you wrote "ugly" or "worthless," then your post-it note can say, "Psalm 139:14 - 'Thank you for making me so wonderfully complex! Your workmanship is marvelous—how well I know it."

- After writing your counteract post-it note, you may post it over the negative word, or erase the word that you wrote before. Either way, keep in mind that you can decide which label you want to carry moving forward; the choice is yours.
- Pray against the negative words that you see, and allow God to change your heart and show you what it is that He sees.

Side Note: I have a mentee who's walking through this process, right now, and every day she goes to the mirror, and tells herself that she loves herself right before she leaves her room. In the beginning, it was tough for her to even look at herself in the mirror, but with time, the tension was released. While it's a beautiful thing to share your story, most of this work will be between you, the mirror and God. Walk this out. You can do it.

3. GET A JOURNAL AND RECORD YOUR PROCESS.

This is for everybody and anybody. Journaling is a great release. It's also great for praying when you can't put things into words. Make sure that you get a journal, recognize, admit, accept, address, and face your truth.

4. Affirmations(Please add your own):
- I AM A JEWEL.
- I AM VALUED.
- I AM LOVED.
- I AM CHERISHED.
- I AM WORTH BEING WAITED ON.
- I AM RESPECTFUL.
- I AM THOUGHT ABOUT.
- I AM GOOD.
- I AM LIGHT.
- I AM A JOY TO BE AROUND.
- I AM WHERE I AM SUPPOSED TO BE.
- GOD'S TIMING IS BEST.
- GOD IS INTENTIONAL.
- I AM PROTECTED.
- IF IT'S NOT FOR ME, THEN IT WON'T BE THERE. IF IT IS FOR ME, THEN IT WILL BE THERE.
- I AM A SERVANT OF THE LORD.
- I AM THE DAUGHTER OF A KING.
- I WILL STAY OUT OF GOD'S WAY IN REFERENCE TO HIS PLANS FOR MY LIFE. MY JOB IS JUST TO WALK IN IT.

5. Book Suggestions(Please add your own):

- Recovery from Rejection (Ryan Lestrange)
- The Father Daughter Talk (R. C. Blakes Jr.)
- Woman Evolve (Sarah Jakes Roberts)

6. Song Suggestions(Please add your own):
   - Move Me - Jaye Little
   - Jireh - Elevation Worship & Maverick City Music; ft. Chandler Moore and Naomi Raine
   - Good and Loved - Travis Greene ft. Steffany Gretzinger
   - Unstoppable - Koryn Hawthorne
   - Out Of Hiding - Tye Tribbett
   - Grateful - Rita Ora
   - You Sustain - Transformation Church
   - I Am Light - India Arie
   - My Everything - Bri Babineaux
   - Bigger Than Me - LeAndria Johnson
   - Free - Brianna Sharpe
   - Make Room - Jonathan McReynolds
   - Dwell Here - Jayy Todd
   - Never Alone - Ja'Myron Smoke
   - Trust You With My Life - Shan Townsend
   - My Portion - Jekalyn Carr

7. Prepare for God to BLOW YOUR MIND!

WOMAN OF WORTH:
I am calling the **<u>REAL YOU</u>** out now.
WE ARE CASTING AWAY
THE OLD SELF,
THE SHAMING SELF,
THE SELF-SABOTAGING SELF,
THE JEALOUS SELF,
THE INSECURE SELF, and
THE OVERTHINKING SELF.

WE ARE NOW CALLING FORTH
THE WHOLE SELF,
THE NEW SELF,
THE BEAUTIFUL SELF,
THE RENEWED SELF,
THE CONFIDENT SELF, and
THE INTELLIGENT SELF.

COME FORTH AND BE WHO GOD HAS
CALLED YOU TO BE
WITHOUT BACKING DOWN,
WITHOUT ALLOWING INTIMIDATION
TO GET IN THE WAY, and

WITHOUT COMPARING YOURSELF TO
ANOTHER, KNOWING THAT YOU ARE
INCOMPARABLE.

WE NOW UNDERSTAND THAT WE
WORK BETTER TOGETHER.
WHERE THERE IS UNITY, THERE IS
STRENGTH.

Pray this prayer:
"LORD, I MAKE ROOM FOR YOU.
HELP ME, LORD, TO SEE ME THE
WAY THAT YOU SEE ME:
WHOLE,
PRECIOUS,
BRILLIANT,
BEAUTIFUL,
SET ASIDE, and
SET APART."

I DECLARE THAT THIS DAY:

- WE SAY "NO" TO <u>FEAR</u>, AND WE SAY "YES" TO <u>FREEDOM</u>!
- WE SAY "NO" TO <u>SELF DOUBT</u>, AND WE SAY "YES" TO <u>SELF CONFIDENCE</u>!
- WE SAY "NO" TO <u>PEER PRESSURE</u>, AND WE SAY "YES" TO <u>GOOD DECISIONS</u>!
- WE SAY "NO" TO <u>OVERTHINKING</u>, AND WE SAY "YES" TO <u>TRUSTING THE PROCESS</u>!

HEY WOMAN OF WORTH,
YOU DID IT, and
YOU'RE DOING IT.
SO KEEP GOING.

THANK YOU LORD FOR RESTORING OUR LIVES, OUR TIME, OUR WORTH, OUR CONFIDENCE, and OUR FUTURE.

GOD, WE TRUST YOU TO MOVE
FORWARD.
HELP US TO REACH AS FAR AS WE
HAVE TO GO.
WOMAN, YOU DON'T HAVE TO WALK
THIS PATH ALONE.
SHARE THIS WITH A FRIEND.
ENCOURAGE A SISTER, TODAY.
WE ARE ALL IN THIS TOGETHER.
ACCOUNTABILITY PARTNERS ARE
NECESSARY.

GOD SAYS,
"I GOT YOU, NOW.
I'M HERE TO RESTORE YOU.
YOU CAN RELEASE, NOW.
I WON'T LET YOU GO.
I WILL NEVER LET YOU GO.
I WILL CHANGE YOU.
I WILL RESTORE YOU.
I WILL TRANSFORM YOU.
I HAVE EVERYTHING THAT YOU
NEED.

I'M HERE TO REBUILD YOU.
I'M HERE TO RENEW YOU.
I'M HERE TO RESTORE YOUR HEART.
I'M HERE TO MEND YOUR BROKEN
HEART.
I'M HERE TO RENEW YOUR MIND.
I'M HERE TO BREAK THE CHAINS.
IT'S TIME TO COME HOME."

SHAKE OFF EVERYTHING THAT YOU
CAN'T TAKE TO YOUR NEXT, WOMAN
OF WORTH.
YOU'VE BEEN HELD DOWN TOO
LONG FROM THINGS THAT NO
LONGER SUIT YOU:
- ANXIETY.
- DEPRESSION.
- YOUR FLESHLY DESIRES.
- YOUR CARNAL WAYS.
- SUICIDAL THOUGHTS.

YOU CAN RELEASE THEM, NOW.

We will not be insecure in this season.
Amen? Okay? Alright. <3
I love you, Beautiful.

ABOUT THE AUTHOR

Jaye Little of Montgomery, Alabama is the founder of A Hope To Help, a non-profit organization aimed to advise, encourage, and support youth who may be hopeless during transitions in life. She is passionate about young people and is currently a singer, marching band auxiliary coordinator, mathematics educator, motivational speaker, and author.

Jaye Little is a woman of God, purpose, beauty, humility and grace. In everything that she does, the glory belongs to God.

Website: jayelittle.org

Keep Up With Us on Social Media:

Facebook: A Hope To Help

Instagram: @ahopetohelp

YouTube: A Hope To Help

Twitter: @AHopeToHelp